IF THE EARTH IS ROUND...

Poems by Brett Fleishman

Illustrations by David Harston

Published by Mindstir Media LLC
45 Lafayette Rd. Suite 181 | North Hampton, NH 03862 | USA
1.800.767.0531 | www.mindstirmedia.com

ISBN-13: 978-0-9991507-7-1
Library of Congress Control Number: 2017911858

In loving memory of my grandfather, Leonard Landau, whose sense of humor I still recall vividly.

Carson,

"Always dream big. It's OK if you do.
If you don't, there's no way that your dream will come true."

Brett Fleishman !!
☺

Table of Contents

LONELY GHOST

Dylan is the kindest ghost this world has ever seen

But, since he looks frightening, kids think he's very mean

Dylan lives a lonely life, accepting this routine

He fits in just once a year. Of course, on Halloween.

MUSICAL INSTRUMENTS

Music lessons are taken on Floor 53

But this building has no elevator, you see

This is fine for the girl playing flute. Her name's Dee.

But it's tough for the boy on piano. Poor Lee.

HOUSE FOR SALE

There's a new house for sale!
There's a new house for sale!
Guess this property just got released
It was not here before
There was dirt, nothing more
Now it sits all alone unpoliced
This house has tons of charm
It once sat on a farm
Such a mystery it costs the least
'Cause it has so much stuff
Way, way more than enough
There is even a witch from the East

UNFORTUNATE IKE

Unfortunate Ike

Never learned how to bike

As a kid but, of course, he survived

His Dad told Ike he may

Wish he'd learned how one day

And it looks like that day has arrived

SCRAGGLY BEARD

Some thought it was weird

When the man with the beard

Kept on growing and growing his hair

'Look at him. He's a slob!'

Said a kid, a real snob

'It's as if the man just doesn't care!'

But these folks never knew

As his beard grew and grew

The old man was completely aware

He was thinking ahead

Now he never leaves bed

Since whatever he needs is right there

SHAKE, RATTLE, NICOLE

Never shake

A rattlesnake

'Cause it will eat you whole

My friend Jake

Made that mistake

I guess so did Nicole

IF THE EARTH IS ROUND...

Teachers claim the Earth is round
But how can this be true?
Children don't fall into space
I guess their shoes have glue!

Cow-Tipping Advice

If you choose to tip a cow
Which I don't recommend
First make sure the ground is flat
Check that her knees can bend
You may need a running start
You'll need speed at the end
Otherwise it tips backwards
Learned Sam, my flattest friend

SHELL-SHOCKED

She sells seashells by the seashore
When the sea swells, she sees shells soar

HERE TO THERE

I'm afraid to step inside a closing elevator

I don't like to climb onto a speeding escalator

So I take the stairs where I am not a hesitator

I am sure the other two have risks that are far greater

Advice For You

If you aren't afraid to fail
I'm sure you will succeed
Even though this poem's short
Please give it one more read

BABY PIPER

What's that sound?

It's all around

I think it's Baby Piper

I hear groans

And whines and moans

She's never quite this hyper

What's that smell?

It's tough to tell

Yuck, it's her stinky diaper!

Since I'm tough

I'll take it off...

But promise me you'll wipe her

GRUMPY ELF

He wraps the gifts. He shines the sleigh.
He works eight hours every day
He has no time to nap or play
So he's a grumpy elf

As Santa rests (he loves to lay)
The elf gets up, then stomps away
While leaving, Santa hears him say
'Go wrap these gifts yourself!'

BEAUTIFUL KITTY

This beautiful kitty

Is playful and pretty

It's furry and has tiny paws

Of course, it's a pity

It scratches a bitty

Did anyone trim kitty's claws?

10-BOOK POEM

You must read my second book
This poem isn't done...

If you read my next beginner book and take the time...
You will see this poem's next two lines, and they will rhyme!

ROLLER COASTER

Welcome, girls! Welcome, boys!

Clap your hands. Make some noise.

You're aboard the best coaster of all!

Four can ride in each group

You will love the last loop

Like the coaster, it's scary and tall

We are starting to go

You'll be happy to know

Every detail's been checked, large and small

Every detail but one

No big deal, you'll have fun

If the coaster survives the first fall

SNORKELING

You should join me snorkeling
Jump in! It's worth a try.
There aren't many fish today
How strange. I wonder why?

LUCKY GIRL

I cough

I burp

I snort

I slurp

I fart

I puke

I pee

So who will be the lucky girl who gets to marry me?

DRAGON FOR HIRE

Come meet my pet dragon

He's healthy and strong

He is looking for work

He's been looking so long

If you need help

Lighting your birthday candles

Give him a call

This he easily handles

HUNGRY TEDDY

This teddy bear just eats and eats. It eats all day and night.
It eats the food of other teddy bears. This isn't right.

This teddy bear is not concerned how other teddies feel
'Give me all your food right now! I want another meal!'

The other teddy bears are scared. They give him all their food.
Once he's eaten everything, he's in an awful mood

'No one cares my belly hurts,' upset, the teddy huffed
They did not and weren't surprised the teddy bear was stuffed

SECRET POEM - I'm a secret poem. You were NOT supposed to find me! Please do not tell anyone. For that, I thank you kindly.

SIMON SAYS

Simon says...put your hand on your hip
Simon says...gently bite on your lip

Simon says...wiggle most of your toes
Simon says... scratch the tip of your nose

Simon says...clench your hand, make a fist
Simon says...rub your knee with your wrist

Simon says... flip this page and you'll lose...

Simon won 'cause you couldn't refuse!

Brett's Bio

Brett Fleishman grew up in the suburbs of Philadelphia. In 1995, he earned his B.A. In 2001, he earned his M.B.A. At no point did he earn a roster spot in the N.B.A. Since 2001, Brett has been living with his two sons, Jacob and Dylan, in the greater Boston area. (Please note that, while Brett and his sons enjoy living in Boston, their sports allegiances remain firmly Philadelphian.)

To learn more about Brett, please check out his bio at www.brettfleishman.com. You can also follow him on Instagram, Twitter, and Facebook.

Also by Brett Fleishman

Twist and Shout! is a compilation of 33 funny-bone-tickling poems designed for intermediate readers. Beware, this book is very punny!

Empty Beaches is a compilation of 25 funny-bone-tickling poems designed for advanced readers. This book is also pretty punny!

CPSIA information can be obtained
at www.ICGtesting.com
Printed in the USA
BVHW02s0444100318
510011BV00002B/2/P

The LAND of CHOCOLATE COSMOS

For my son, Ryan,
who gave me my first glance inside
a five year old boy's imagination...love you.

The Land Of Chocolate Cosmos

© 2010, Suzie Canale

Printed in the United States.

PRT1210A

ISBN-13: 978-1-936319-28-2
ISBN-10: 1-936319-28-4

Mascot Books
560 Herndon Parkway #120, Herndon, VA 20170

www.mascotbooks.com

In a land very far away,
where no place is quite the same
was a town made out of chocolate,
"Land of Cosmos" was its name.

Now this town could be quite common,
To most you may already know
except a magical flower grew there,
called the enchanted chocolate cosmos.

The faces of the flower,
revealed a rich mahogany hue,
that held a characteristic,
which might really interest you.

Within its burgundy dark petals,
contained a spell within its scent,
that turned everything to chocolate,
wherever the sweet aroma went.

The town was completely covered,
with the fragrance of the bloom,
drifting miles in every direction,
from the fields up to the moon.

There were trees with bon-bon apples,
stars made from chocolate dots,
that would light the way for townsfolk,
twinkling their sugary white spots.

The rivers bubbled over,
with a creamy chocolate brew,
that would entice the little children,
to stick their fingers in the goo.

Clouds were chocolate cotton candy,
until they rained down chocolate chips.
People squealed with sheer delight,
when they touched their cherry lips.

The cosmos was very important,
for it brought a lucrative fame,
found within the "sweet tooth" business,
where the town had earned its name.

People would travel from far off places,
to taste a mouth watering treat,
made from the powerful cosmos petals,
at prices you couldn't beat!

The magic from the flower,
brought an incredible burst of flavor,
to whomever ate the goodies,
every last bite they would savor.

Endless shelves of chocolate cookies,
chocolate bars and chocolate pie,
chocolate brownies, fudge and cupcakes
something for everyone to buy.

They sold hundreds of chocolate kisses,
chocolate pops and chocolate tarts,
chocolate raisins, chocolate pretzels,
chocolate valentine's shaped hearts.

There were even fruits for dipping,
In a milky rich fondue,
Strawberries, bananas, and even apples,
grapes, papaya and mangos, too.

Things seemed so picture perfect,
as the stems went faster and faster,
but a little boy named Coco,
recognized a recycling disaster.

Now Coco was only five,
but was wise beyond his years,
noticed the depleting amount of cosmos,
becoming his greatest of all fears.

Coco had always appreciated nature,
within everything She grew,
and conserving our natural resources,
was something that all of us should do.

So he began to investigate further,
to seek out what he could find,
and after snooping around in all the shops,
what he saw just blew his mind!

For what he found had proven,
the merchants would stand the accused,
because there were hundreds of discarded petals,
thrown away and never used.

Instead of using all the flower,
they had only plucked a piece,
then left the rest for garbage,
before the petals could release.

A waste was what it simply was,
there was no other way to see.
So Coco went off to warn the townsfolk,
of the approaching tragedy.

He said, "We all need to try to conserve
or the end will surely be near."
But the shopkeepers ignored him and only replied,
"There are plenty of cosmos here!"

So no sooner did they forget the words,
of Coco's speech to warn,
did the flowers begin to vanish from fields,
few new stems of cosmos were born.

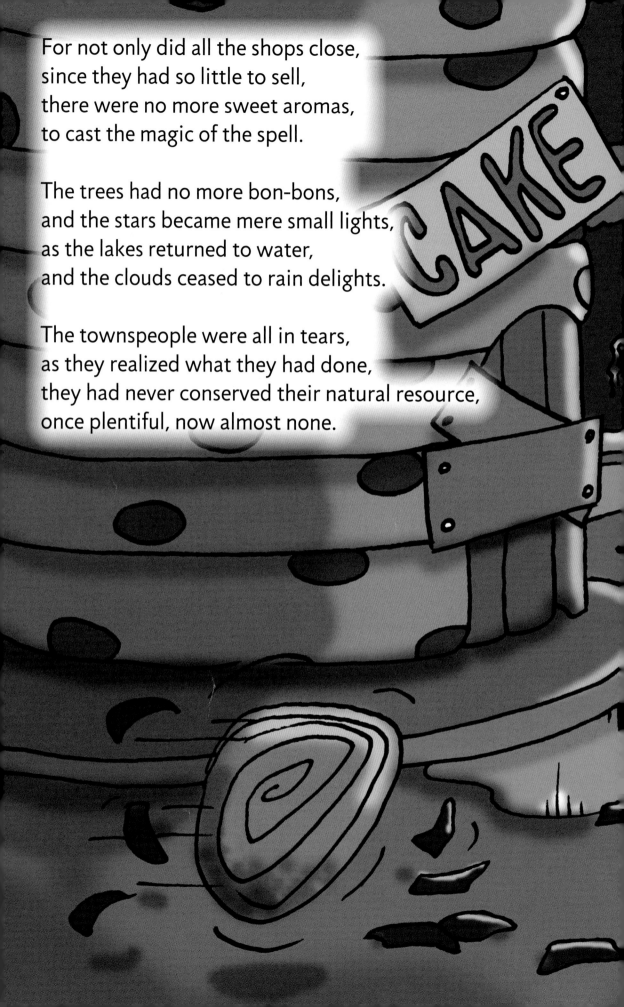

For not only did all the shops close,
since they had so little to sell,
there were no more sweet aromas,
to cast the magic of the spell.

The trees had no more bon-bons,
and the stars became mere small lights,
as the lakes returned to water,
and the clouds ceased to rain delights.

The townspeople were all in tears,
as they realized what they had done,
they had never conserved their natural resource,
once plentiful, now almost none.

But Coco had learned a method,
on how to cultivate and grow,
an endangered species in the wild,
he could save the chocolate cosmos!

He began to explain to everyone,
what they simply needed to do,
split one plant's roots in half, replant,
and one would soon be two.

So that's exactly what they did,
they dug and hoped the crop regrew,
they worked all day and prayed all night,
that their fields would grow anew.

But soon they had to realize,
they needed help from all around,
if anyone were to see the cosmos
once again cover the ground.

And then it came to Coco,
an idea which was very clever,
ask all the people from miles around,
to join in the "green" endeavor!

They would learn about recycling,
and conservation of the land.
to learn to save our natural resources,
and to lend a helping hand.

Soon the fields grew back their cosmos,
life returned to normalcy,
except a land once known for chocolate,
was known now for "Green Policy."

The Chocolate Cosmos

The chocolate cosmos is native to the country of Mexico and is uniquely known for its unusual characteristics. The flower's scent, color and natural delicacy has made it one of the trendier flowers of today. The cosmos is popularly seen in many fine gothic gardens as an essential piece to the puzzle palette. Cosmos are seen more and more throughout the wedding industry placed in floral centerpieces and bridal bouquets. The dainty flowers are also used as decoration on cakes and as accents in the brides' hair.

The perennial is famously known for its unmistaken fragrance described as having either a vanilla or chocolate aroma. The petals of the flower are painted in either a rich mahogany, burgundy or chocolate toned color. Often they are described as merlot in hue. The petals are clustered around their slender stem which may or may not have multiple shoots or blooms. Typically, the stems range from six to ten inches long depending on the variety.

The cosmos is classified as an endangered species in the wild. It is a rare flower because it cannot duplicate itself in the soil. The only way to recultivate the plant is to split apart the root system and replant in well draining soil. It is grown best in warm temperatures and is one of the few flowers that prefer less water to more. The cosmos blooms from summer to early fall and can be wintered by repotting and placing in a warm sunlit area of the home.

About the Author

Suzie Hearl Canale grew up in Andover, Massachusetts and is a graduate of Salem State College. She began her career as a children's book author after a twenty five year career in the wholesale floral industry in Boston where she was inspired by flowers named after child friendly foods. She developed the concept of *The Bean Town Tales* which are a series of books geared towards educating and empowering children to make positive changes within the key concerns of our society. "The Land of Chocolate Cosmos" is the first installation of the "Green" series, which focuses on the importance of conservation within the environment. Currently residing in Chestnut Hill, Massachusetts, she is also busily raising her two sons and participating in Mass Bay's Disaster Assistance Chapter of the American Red Cross.

Have a book idea? Contact us at:
Mascot Books
P.O. Box 220157
Chantilly, VA 20153-0157
info@mascotbooks.com

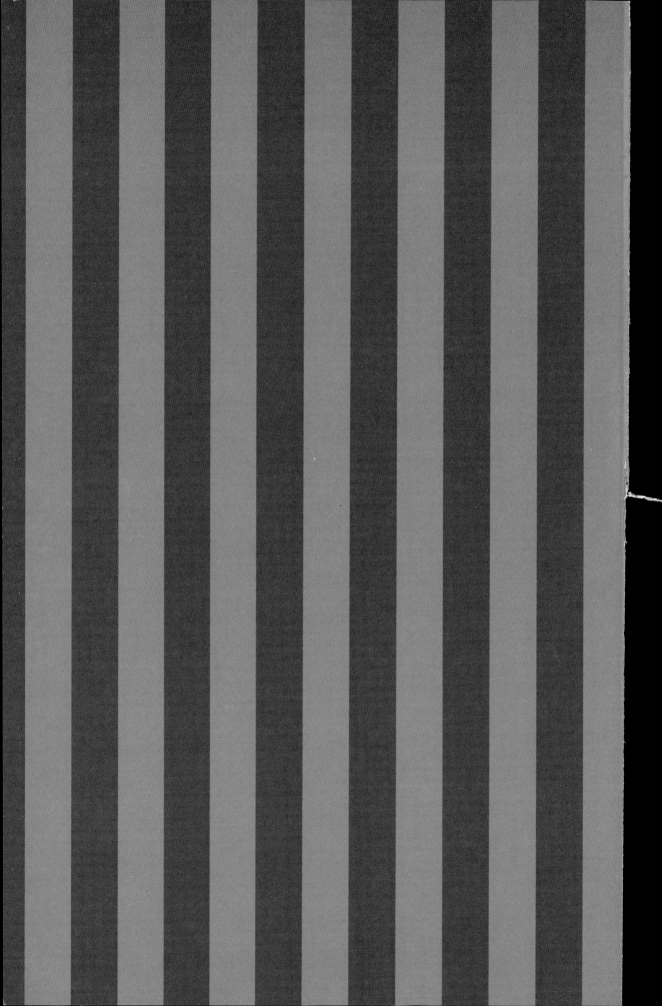